EMMANUEL JOSEPH

Governance and Growth, The Hidden Link Between Political Systems and Business Success

Copyright © 2025 by Emmanuel Joseph

All rights reserved. No part of this publication may be reproduced, stored or transmitted in any form or by any means, electronic, mechanical, photocopying, recording, scanning, or otherwise without written permission from the publisher. It is illegal to copy this book, post it to a website, or distribute it by any other means without permission.

First edition

This book was professionally typeset on Reedsy.
Find out more at reedsy.com

Contents

1. Chapter 1: Introduction — 1
2. Chapter 2: Historical Evolution of Governance and Business — 3
3. Chapter 3: The Role of Democracy in Economic Development — 5
4. Chapter 5: Corruption, Transparency, and Business Growth — 7
5. Chapter 6: Impact of Political Stability on Business... — 9
6. Chapter 7: Regulatory Frameworks and Entrepreneurial Growth — 11
7. Chapter 8: Globalization and Political Systems: A... — 13
8. Chapter 9: Case Studies of High-Growth Economies and Their... — 15
9. Chapter 10: Challenges in Aligning Political and Business... — 17
10. Chapter 11: Future Trends: Political Systems and Business... — 19
11. Chapter 12: Conclusion — 21
12. Chapter 13: The Role of Institutions in Shaping Economic... — 23
13. Chapter 14: The Impact of Social Movements on Governance and... — 25
14. Chapter 15: The Role of International Organizations in... — 27
15. Chapter 16: The Influence of Culture on Governance and... — 29
16. Chapter 17: The Role of Education in Shaping Political... — 31

1

Chapter 1: Introduction

In the intricate tapestry of human civilization, governance and business have always been interwoven threads. The evolution of political systems has consistently influenced the economic trajectory of nations. From ancient monarchies to modern democracies, the interplay between political authority and economic prosperity has shaped societies and driven progress. Understanding the hidden link between governance and business success requires a deep dive into the historical, sociopolitical, and economic dimensions that define this relationship.

The purpose of this book is to uncover the nuanced connections between political systems and business growth. While it is widely acknowledged that governance impacts economic performance, the specific mechanisms through which this occurs are often shrouded in complexity. By exploring different political systems and their influence on business environments, this book aims to provide a comprehensive understanding of how governance shapes economic outcomes.

At the heart of this exploration lies the question: Why do some political systems foster robust business growth while others impede it? Is it the inherent qualities of the political system, the policies they implement, or the cultural and social context in which they operate? These questions are crucial for policymakers, business leaders, and scholars seeking to navigate the ever-changing landscape of global economics.

By examining historical precedents, contemporary examples, and theoretical frameworks, this book will shed light on the multifaceted relationship between governance and business success. It will draw upon a range of disciplines, including political science, economics, sociology, and history, to provide a holistic view of how political systems influence economic growth. The insights gained from this exploration will not only enhance our understanding of past and present dynamics but also offer valuable lessons for shaping future policies and strategies.

2

Chapter 2: Historical Evolution of Governance and Business

The relationship between governance and business has evolved through centuries, each era marked by distinct political and economic structures. In ancient times, monarchies and empires dominated the political landscape. Kings and emperors wielded absolute power, and their policies directly influenced commerce and trade. Ancient Egypt, Rome, and China are prime examples where centralized authority facilitated the establishment of vast trading networks and infrastructural advancements that boosted economic activity.

As the feudal system emerged in medieval Europe, the decentralization of power created a complex web of allegiances and economic dependencies. Landlords and vassals became crucial players in the economic realm, with local governance impacting agricultural production and trade. The rise of city-states in Italy, such as Venice and Florence, demonstrated how republican governance could foster vibrant mercantile economies, setting the stage for the Renaissance's commercial boom.

The Industrial Revolution marked a turning point in the governance-business nexus. The emergence of nation-states and the shift towards more democratic forms of governance provided the political stability needed for industrialization. Governments began to implement policies that encouraged innovation, protected property rights, and facilitated market expansion. The correlation between political reforms and economic growth during this period underscores the importance of governance in shaping business success.

In the contemporary era, the global political economy is characterized by diverse governance systems ranging from democracies to autocracies. The interplay between these systems and their respective business environments continues to shape the economic destinies of nations. Understanding the historical evolution of this relationship provides valuable insights into the factors that drive economic growth and the potential for future development.

3

Chapter 3: The Role of Democracy in Economic Development

Democracy, as a system of governance, is often lauded for its potential to promote economic development. The principle of political equality, where citizens have a voice in decision-making, creates a framework for accountability and transparency. Democratic institutions, such as free and fair elections, independent judiciaries, and a free press, play a crucial role in fostering an environment conducive to business growth.

One of the key advantages of democracy is the protection of property rights. In democratic societies, legal frameworks are established to ensure that businesses can operate without fear of arbitrary expropriation. This legal certainty encourages investment and innovation, driving economic growth. Furthermore, democratic governance promotes the rule of law, reducing corruption and creating a level playing field for all market participants.

Democracies also tend to have more inclusive economic policies. By prioritizing education, healthcare, and social welfare, democratic governments invest in human capital, which is essential for sustained economic growth. Moreover, the pluralistic nature of democracies allows for a diversity of ideas and perspectives, fostering a culture of entrepreneurship and innovation.

However, the relationship between democracy and economic development is not without challenges. Political instability, partisan conflicts, and short-term policy focus can hinder economic progress. Despite these challenges, the overall impact of democratic governance on economic development remains positive, as it creates an environment where businesses can thrive, innovate, and contribute to national prosperity.

Chapter 4: Autocracies and Business Success: Myths vs. Reality

Autocratic regimes, characterized by centralized power and limited political freedoms, have often been associated with rapid economic growth. The perception that autocracies can implement long-term economic policies without the constraints of democratic processes has led to debates on the efficacy of different governance systems in promoting business success. However, the reality is more nuanced.

One of the main arguments in favor of autocracies is their ability to maintain political stability and implement economic reforms swiftly. Countries like China and Singapore are frequently cited as examples where autocratic governance has led to impressive economic growth. In these cases, the government's ability to plan and execute large-scale infrastructure projects and industrial policies has created a favorable business environment.

However, the success of autocracies is not uniform. Many authoritarian regimes struggle with corruption, inefficiency, and lack of accountability. The concentration of power in the hands of a few can lead to policy decisions that favor a select group of elites, stifling competition and innovation. Moreover, the absence of political freedoms can result in social unrest and instability, which ultimately hampers economic growth.

While autocracies can achieve short-term economic gains, their long-term sustainability is often questionable. The lack of mechanisms for peaceful power transitions and limited public participation in governance can create vulnerabilities that undermine economic progress. Therefore, the myth of autocratic efficiency must be critically examined in the context of broader governance and economic indicators.

4

Chapter 5: Corruption, Transparency, and Business Growth

Corruption remains one of the most significant challenges to business growth, particularly in developing countries. When public officials abuse their power for private gain, it creates an uneven playing field, distorts markets, and hinders economic development. Businesses may be forced to pay bribes to secure contracts or navigate bureaucratic hurdles, increasing operational costs and discouraging investment.

Transparency in governance is the antidote to corruption. Transparent governments ensure that their actions and decisions are open to public scrutiny, which helps build trust and confidence among businesses and investors. Mechanisms such as public disclosures, anti-corruption agencies, and whistleblower protections are essential in promoting transparency and accountability.

The relationship between transparency and business growth is evident in countries with strong governance frameworks. In these nations, businesses can operate with confidence, knowing that rules and regulations are applied fairly and consistently. This predictability reduces risks and attracts both domestic and foreign investments. Moreover, transparent governance fosters innovation by creating an environment where businesses can compete based on merit rather than connections.

However, achieving transparency is a complex and ongoing process. It requires a commitment to institutional reforms, the active participation of civil society, and a culture of ethical behavior. While some countries have made significant strides in reducing corruption and enhancing transparency, others continue to struggle. The impact of these efforts on business growth underscores the critical role of governance in shaping economic outcomes.

5

Chapter 6: Impact of Political Stability on Business Environment

Political stability is a cornerstone of a thriving business environment. Stable political systems provide the certainty that businesses need to plan and invest for the long term. When governments are stable, they can implement consistent policies, maintain law and order, and create an environment conducive to economic activity. Conversely, political instability, characterized by frequent changes in government, civil unrest, or armed conflict, poses significant risks to businesses.

In countries with stable political systems, businesses can focus on growth and innovation rather than navigating an unpredictable landscape. Stable governance attracts foreign direct investment (FDI) as investors are assured that their investments are secure and that the business environment is reliable. Furthermore, political stability fosters the development of infrastructure, such as transportation networks and communication systems, which are essential for business operations.

However, political stability is not synonymous with authoritarianism. Democratic nations that experience frequent elections and peaceful transitions of power can also achieve high levels of stability. The key is the presence of robust institutions that uphold the rule of law and ensure continuity in governance. For example, countries like Germany and Canada have stable political systems that support a strong business environment while maintaining democratic values.

On the other hand, countries plagued by political instability face significant economic challenges. Businesses in such environments must contend with uncertainties that can disrupt operations, reduce profitability, and deter investment. The impact of political stability on the business environment highlights the importance of governance in fostering economic growth and prosperity.

6

Chapter 7: Regulatory Frameworks and Entrepreneurial Growth

Regulatory frameworks play a crucial role in shaping the business landscape. Well-designed regulations protect consumers, ensure fair competition, and promote sustainable practices. However, overly stringent or poorly implemented regulations can stifle entrepreneurial growth and innovation. The balance between regulation and business freedom is a delicate one, and different political systems approach it in varied ways.

In democratic countries, regulatory frameworks are often developed through a participatory process involving multiple stakeholders, including businesses, consumers, and civil society. This inclusiveness helps ensure that regulations are fair, transparent, and aligned with the needs of the market. For example, environmental regulations that promote sustainable practices can drive innovation in green technologies and create new business opportunities.

Conversely, in autocratic regimes, regulatory frameworks may be imposed top-down with limited input from stakeholders. While this can lead to swift implementation, it may also result in regulations that are out of touch with market realities or that favor certain groups over others. The lack of transparency and accountability in such systems can create an environment where businesses must navigate a maze of bureaucratic hurdles and unofficial fees.

Effective regulatory frameworks strike a balance between protecting public interests and fostering a dynamic business environment. They provide clarity and predictability, reduce barriers to entry, and encourage entrepreneurship. For example, countries with streamlined business registration processes and supportive tax policies tend to see higher rates of new business formation and innovation.

Ultimately, the design and implementation of regulatory frameworks are critical determinants of entrepreneurial growth. By fostering an environment that encourages innovation, reduces barriers, and promotes fair competition, governance systems can significantly influence the success of businesses and the overall economic health of a nation.

7

Chapter 8: Globalization and Political Systems: A Double-Edged Sword

Globalization has transformed the way businesses operate, creating new opportunities and challenges. The integration of global markets has allowed businesses to expand their reach, access new customers, and benefit from economies of scale. However, globalization also exposes businesses to a complex web of political and economic forces that vary across different governance systems.

For businesses operating in multiple countries, understanding the political landscape of each market is crucial. Democratic nations may offer stable and transparent environments, but they also come with regulatory complexities and political risks associated with policy changes and elections. In contrast, autocratic regimes may provide a more predictable environment in the short term but pose risks related to sudden policy shifts, corruption, and political instability.

Globalization has also increased the interdependence of nations, making businesses more vulnerable to geopolitical events. Trade wars, economic sanctions, and diplomatic conflicts can disrupt supply chains, impact market access, and create uncertainty for businesses. Navigating this global landscape requires businesses to develop strategies that account for political risks and leverage opportunities across different governance systems.

The rise of multinational corporations (MNCs) has further highlighted the need for businesses to engage with diverse political systems. MNCs must navigate varying regulatory frameworks, labor standards, and cultural contexts while maintaining ethical practices and corporate social responsibility. This complexity underscores the importance of understanding the hidden link between political systems and business success in a globalized world.

The double-edged sword of globalization presents both opportunities and challenges for businesses. By recognizing the influence of political systems on global markets, businesses can develop strategies that mitigate risks, capitalize on opportunities, and drive sustainable growth in an interconnected world.

8

Chapter 9: Case Studies of High-Growth Economies and Their Political Systems

To understand the hidden link between political systems and business success, it is essential to examine real-world examples of high-growth economies. This chapter delves into case studies of countries that have achieved remarkable economic growth and explores how their political systems have influenced this success.

China: Over the past few decades, China's transformation from an agrarian economy to a global economic powerhouse has been nothing short of extraordinary. Under its autocratic regime, China has implemented sweeping economic reforms, opened up to foreign investment, and developed world-class infrastructure. The central government's ability to plan and execute long-term economic strategies has played a crucial role in this growth. However, China's political system also faces challenges, such as corruption and lack of political freedoms, which may impact its long-term sustainability.

Germany: As one of Europe's largest economies, Germany's success can be attributed to its stable democratic governance, robust legal framework, and emphasis on innovation. The country's strong institutions, efficient regulatory environment, and commitment to social welfare have created a conducive atmosphere for business growth. Germany's ability to balance economic competitiveness with social equity underscores the importance of inclusive governance in driving sustainable development.

Singapore: Singapore is a prime example of how a city-state with limited natural resources can achieve remarkable economic success through strategic governance. Under an authoritarian regime, Singapore has developed a highly efficient bureaucracy, world-class infrastructure, and a favorable business environment. The government's focus on education, innovation, and trade has propelled Singapore to become a global financial hub. However, the lack of political freedoms and concerns over civil liberties remain points of contention.

South Korea: South Korea's rapid economic development, known as the "Miracle on the Han River," showcases the impact of effective governance on business success. The country's transition from military rule to a vibrant democracy has been accompanied by significant economic reforms, technological advancements, and a strong export-oriented economy. South Korea's ability to foster innovation and support key industries, such as electronics and automotive, has been instrumental in its growth.

These case studies highlight the diverse ways in which political systems can influence business success. While each country has its unique context, common themes such as effective governance, investment in human capital, and strategic economic planning emerge as key drivers of growth.

9

Chapter 10: Challenges in Aligning Political and Business Interests

Aligning political and business interests is a complex and often contentious process. While both political leaders and business executives aim for economic growth and development, their approaches and priorities can differ significantly. This chapter explores the challenges in achieving a harmonious relationship between governance and business.

One of the primary challenges is the conflict of interest between short-term political goals and long-term business strategies. Politicians, especially in democratic systems, may focus on policies that yield immediate benefits to gain public support and secure re-election. In contrast, businesses often require stable and predictable policies to plan for the future and make significant investments.

Regulatory burdens also pose a challenge. Governments may implement regulations to protect consumers, ensure fair competition, and address social and environmental concerns. However, businesses may view these regulations as impediments to growth and profitability. Striking a balance between necessary regulations and business freedom is essential to fostering a conducive business environment.

Corruption and rent-seeking behavior further complicate the alignment of political and business interests. When political leaders and officials engage in corrupt practices, it distorts the market and undermines fair competition. Businesses may be forced to engage in unethical practices to secure contracts or navigate bureaucratic obstacles, ultimately harming the overall economy.

Additionally, the global nature of modern businesses presents challenges in aligning political and business interests. Multinational corporations operate across multiple jurisdictions, each with its own political and regulatory environment. Navigating these diverse landscapes requires businesses to develop strategies that account for political risks and leverage opportunities while maintaining ethical standards.

Addressing these challenges requires a collaborative approach, where political leaders and business executives work together to create an environment that supports sustainable economic growth. By fostering dialogue, promoting transparency, and ensuring accountability, it is possible to align political and business interests for the benefit of society as a whole.

10

Chapter 11: Future Trends: Political Systems and Business Growth

As the world continues to evolve, several future trends will shape the relationship between political systems and business growth. Understanding these trends is crucial for policymakers, business leaders, and scholars to navigate the complexities of the global economy.

Digital Transformation: The rapid advancement of technology and digital transformation will have profound implications for governance and business. Governments will need to adapt to new technologies, such as artificial intelligence, blockchain, and the Internet of Things, to create regulatory frameworks that promote innovation while protecting public interests. Businesses that embrace digital transformation will be better positioned to thrive in the evolving landscape.

Sustainability and Climate Change: The growing emphasis on sustainability and addressing climate change will impact both governance and business practices. Governments will implement policies to promote renewable energy, reduce carbon emissions, and encourage sustainable practices. Businesses that prioritize sustainability and adopt green technologies will gain a competitive edge and contribute to a more sustainable future.

Geopolitical Shifts: Geopolitical shifts, such as the rise of emerging economies, changes in trade policies, and regional conflicts, will influence the global business environment. Political leaders and businesses must be prepared to navigate these shifts by developing strategies that mitigate risks and capitalize on new opportunities.

Social Equity and Inclusion: The increasing focus on social equity and inclusion will shape governance and business practices. Governments will implement policies to address income inequality, promote diversity, and ensure equal opportunities for all citizens. Businesses that prioritize social responsibility and create inclusive workplaces will enhance their reputation and attract talent.

Global Health and Pandemics: The COVID-19 pandemic has highlighted the importance of global health and resilience. Governments and businesses must collaborate to enhance healthcare systems, develop pandemic preparedness plans, and ensure the continuity of essential services. The experience of managing pandemics will shape future governance and business strategies.

By understanding these future trends, political leaders and business executives can develop strategies that promote sustainable economic growth and address the challenges of the evolving global landscape.

11

Chapter 12: Conclusion

The relationship between governance and business growth is complex and multifaceted. Political systems, whether democratic or autocratic, play a crucial role in shaping the business environment and influencing economic outcomes. By examining historical precedents, contemporary examples, and future trends, this book has aimed to uncover the hidden link between political systems and business success.

Governance matters. The effectiveness of political institutions, the transparency of government actions, and the stability of the political environment all impact business growth and economic development. While different political systems have their strengths and weaknesses, the key is to create an environment that fosters innovation, protects property rights, and promotes fair competition.

The insights gained from this exploration can inform policymakers, business leaders, and scholars in their efforts to drive sustainable economic growth. By aligning political and business interests, promoting transparency and accountability, and embracing future trends, it is possible to create a prosperous and inclusive economy.

The journey of understanding the hidden link between governance and growth is ongoing. As the world continues to evolve, new challenges and opportunities will emerge. By remaining vigilant, adaptive, and committed to ethical practices, it is possible to navigate the complexities of the global economy and build a brighter future for all.

12

Chapter 13: The Role of Institutions in Shaping Economic Outcomes

Institutions, both formal and informal, are the backbone of any political system. Formal institutions include constitutions, laws, regulations, and governmental structures, while informal institutions encompass social norms, cultural practices, and traditions. Together, they shape the business environment and influence economic outcomes.

Strong institutions provide a stable framework for economic activities by enforcing property rights, ensuring contract enforcement, and promoting fair competition. For example, an independent judiciary plays a critical role in resolving disputes and maintaining the rule of law, which is essential for business confidence and investment. Similarly, regulatory agencies that operate transparently and impartially create a level playing field for businesses, fostering competition and innovation.

In contrast, weak institutions can hinder economic growth. Corruption, bureaucratic inefficiencies, and lack of accountability erode trust in the system, discourage investment, and stifle entrepreneurial activities. Businesses may face unpredictable regulatory environments, frequent policy changes, and unfair practices that create barriers to growth.

The effectiveness of institutions is closely linked to the quality of governance. Countries with strong, transparent, and accountable institutions tend to perform better economically. Understanding the role of institutions in shaping economic outcomes is crucial for policymakers and business leaders aiming to create a conducive environment for sustainable growth.

13

Chapter 14: The Impact of Social Movements on Governance and Business

Social movements have historically played a significant role in shaping governance and business practices. These movements, driven by collective action, aim to address social, economic, and political injustices. They can influence policy changes, alter public perceptions, and drive business practices towards more ethical and inclusive standards.

One notable example is the labor movement, which has had a profound impact on workers' rights and business practices worldwide. Through collective bargaining and advocacy, labor unions have secured better wages, working conditions, and benefits for workers. This, in turn, has led to more equitable distribution of wealth and improved living standards.

Environmental movements have also had a significant influence on governance and business. Advocacy for sustainable practices, climate action, and environmental protection has resulted in the implementation of green policies and regulations. Businesses are increasingly adopting sustainable practices, recognizing the importance of environmental stewardship and corporate social responsibility.

Civil rights movements, such as the fight for racial and gender equality, have driven significant changes in governance and business practices. Policies promoting diversity, equity, and inclusion have become integral to modern businesses, fostering innovation and creating more inclusive workplaces.

Social movements continue to shape the political and business landscape. By advocating for change, raising awareness, and holding institutions accountable, these movements play a crucial role in driving progress and ensuring that governance and business practices align with societal values.

14

Chapter 15: The Role of International Organizations in Governance and Business

International organizations, such as the United Nations, World Trade Organization, International Monetary Fund, and World Bank, play a vital role in shaping governance and business practices globally. These organizations set standards, provide guidance, and facilitate cooperation among nations to address global challenges and promote economic development.

The United Nations (UN) promotes peace, security, and human rights, creating a stable environment for business activities. The UN's Sustainable Development Goals (SDGs) provide a comprehensive framework for addressing global challenges, including poverty, inequality, and environmental sustainability. Businesses aligning their practices with the SDGs contribute to achieving these goals while benefiting from a more stable and equitable global environment.

The World Trade Organization (WTO) facilitates international trade by establishing rules and resolving trade disputes. By promoting open and fair trade, the WTO helps businesses access global markets, fostering economic growth and development. However, trade policies and agreements must balance the interests of various stakeholders to ensure fair competition and protect domestic industries.

The International Monetary Fund (IMF) and World Bank provide financial assistance, technical expertise, and policy advice to countries facing economic challenges. By supporting economic stability and development, these organizations create a conducive environment for business growth. However, their policies and interventions must consider the unique context and needs of each country to ensure sustainable outcomes.

International organizations play a critical role in shaping global governance and business practices. By fostering cooperation, setting standards, and addressing global challenges, these organizations contribute to a more stable and prosperous world.

15

Chapter 16: The Influence of Culture on Governance and Business

Culture, encompassing values, beliefs, norms, and practices, profoundly influences governance and business. Cultural context shapes how political systems operate, how businesses interact with stakeholders, and how economic activities are conducted.

In collectivist cultures, such as those in many Asian countries, there is a strong emphasis on community, harmony, and group cohesion. These cultural values influence governance by promoting consensus-based decision-making and social stability. Businesses in collectivist cultures often prioritize long-term relationships, loyalty, and collaboration, fostering trust and cooperation.

In contrast, individualistic cultures, such as those in Western countries, emphasize personal freedom, autonomy, and individual rights. Democratic governance systems in these cultures prioritize individual participation, political equality, and accountability. Businesses in individualistic cultures often prioritize innovation, competition, and personal achievement, driving economic dynamism and entrepreneurial growth.

Culture also influences attitudes toward corruption, transparency, and regulatory compliance. In cultures with high levels of trust and social capital, there is often greater compliance with laws and regulations, promoting a fair and transparent business environment. Conversely, in cultures with low trust and high power distance, corruption and informal practices may be more prevalent, posing challenges to governance and business.

Understanding the influence of culture on governance and business is essential for policymakers and business leaders operating in diverse contexts. By recognizing cultural nuances and adapting strategies accordingly, it is possible to create more effective governance systems and business practices that align with cultural values and promote sustainable growth.

16

Chapter 17: The Role of Education in Shaping Political Systems and Business Success

Education is a fundamental driver of both governance and business success. An educated populace is better equipped to participate in democratic processes, hold leaders accountable, and contribute to informed decision-making. Additionally, education fosters innovation, entrepreneurship, and economic growth by equipping individuals with the skills and knowledge needed to succeed in the modern economy.

In democratic societies, education promotes political engagement and civic responsibility. Educated citizens are more likely to vote, advocate for their rights, and participate in community activities. This active engagement strengthens democratic institutions, promotes transparency, and ensures that governance reflects the will of the people.

Education also plays a critical role in developing human capital, which is essential for business success. Countries with strong education systems produce a skilled and adaptable workforce, driving innovation and productivity. Businesses benefit from a talent pool that can navigate complex challenges, embrace new technologies, and contribute to sustainable growth.

Moreover, education fosters a culture of lifelong learning and continuous improvement. In rapidly changing economies, businesses must adapt to new trends, technologies, and market demands. An educated workforce that values continuous learning is better positioned to drive innovation and maintain competitiveness.

Investing in education is crucial for both governance and business. By prioritizing quality education, governments can promote political stability, social equity, and economic prosperity. Businesses, in turn, can support education initiatives and develop programs that enhance workforce skills, contributing to a virtuous cycle of growth and development.

Description

In "Governance and Growth: The Hidden Link Between Political Systems and Business Success," the intricate relationship between political structures and economic outcomes is brought to light. This compelling book delves into how different forms of governance—ranging from democracies to autocracies—affect business environments and drive economic growth.

Exploring historical contexts, theoretical frameworks, and contemporary examples, the book uncovers the nuanced connections between governance and business success. Readers will journey through the evolution of political and economic systems, examining how monarchies, democracies, and autocracies have shaped the business landscape over centuries.

The book highlights the advantages and challenges posed by various political systems, addressing critical topics such as corruption, transparency, political stability, and regulatory frameworks. Through insightful case studies of high-growth economies like China, Germany, Singapore, and South Korea, the book provides real-world examples of how governance influences economic prosperity.

Additionally, the book looks ahead to future trends, including digital transformation, sustainability, geopolitical shifts, and social equity, offering valuable insights for policymakers, business leaders, and scholars. By understanding the hidden link between political systems and business growth, readers will gain a deeper appreciation of the factors that drive economic success and the strategies needed to navigate the complexities of the global economy.

www.ingramcontent.com/pod-product-compliance
Lightning Source LLC
LaVergne TN
LVHW020500080526
838202LV00057B/6075